Seawat

by
Tony So
and
Noel Cu

Published for the National Trust
by
Dinosaur Publications Ltd
Over, Cambridge, Great Britain
© Tony Soper & Noel Cusa 1978   ISBN 0/85122/130/0

These pictures show the two faces of the sea; on the calmest of sunlit days and on a day of wild storm. But whatever the weather, the sea is a source of endless interest. At first glance it may seem no more than a giant puddle, featureless and flat. But beneath the surface there's a jungle of life. Even the colour of the sea changes. On a clear day, off the coast of Devon or Cornwall, it may be the deepest of blues shading to azure in the shallows. Yet when clouds obscure the sun and the sky darkens, that same sea looks green. Off North Sea coasts and near estuaries the colour is more sombre, affected by great quantities of silt suspended in the water.

Look at the horizon. Sometimes, just before or after a rainstorm, there will be a sharp line between dark sea and pale sky. In settled hazy weather, the horizon may disappear altogether where the sea and sky merge. In stormy weather great waves may make the line irregular. In calm weather, when the sea is 'as smooth as a mill-pond', the clouds or the setting sun may be reflected in it. But usually, waves shatter the mirror surface, and when the waves are large enough to break, the sea will be flecked with 'white horses'.

The sea is not just a watery desert, but a vital part of our planet's life-support system. It is the source of the rain which waters the land and brings life to the soil and it provides us with quantities of food in return for the steady supply of nutrients which flow down from the land.

This book is intended to help in understanding about the variety of life in the sea. It is for people who like to stand on cliff tops and watch the wheeling seabirds, and for those who sail on the sea and meet strange creatures there.

BEAUFORT WIND SCALE

Force	Wind Speed (knots)	Description	State of the Sea	Probable Height of Waves (metres)	Probable Maximum Wave Height (metres)
0	Less than 1	Calm	Sea like a mirror	—	—
1	1—3	Light air	Ripples with the appearance of scales are formed but without foam crests.	—	—
2	4—6	Light breeze	Small wavelets, still short but more pronounced. Crests have a glassy appearance and do not break.	0·15	0·30
3	7—10	Gentle breeze	Large wavelets. Crests begin to break. Foam of glassy appearance. Perhaps scattered white horses.	0·60	1·0
4	11—16	Moderate breeze	Small waves, becoming larger: fairly frequent horses.	1·0	1·50
5	17—21	Fresh breeze	Moderate waves, taking a more pronounced long form; many white horses are formed. (Chance of some spray).	1·80	2·50
6	22—27	Strong breeze	Large waves begin to form; the white foam crests are more extensive everywhere. (Probably some spray).	3·0	4·0
7	28—33	Near gale	Sea heaps up and white foam from breaking waves begins to be blown in streaks along the direction of the wind.	4·0	6·0
8	34—40	Gale	Moderately high waves of greater length; edges of crests begin to break into spindrift. The foam is blown in well-marked streaks along the direction of the wind.	5·50	7·50
9	41—47	Strong gale	High waves. Dense streaks of foam along the direction of the wind. Crests of waves begin to topple, tumble and roll over. Spray may affect visibility.	7·0	9·75
10	48—55	Storm	Very high waves with long overhanging crests. The resulting foam in great patches is blown in dense white streaks along the direction of the wind. On the whole the surface of the sea takes a white appearance. The tumbling of the sea becomes heavy and shocklike. Visibility affected.	9·0	12·50
11	56—63	Violent storm	Exceptionally high waves. (Small and medium-sized ships might be for a time lost to view behind the waves). The sea is completely covered with long white patches of foam lying along the direction of the wind. Everywhere the edges of the wave crests are blown into froth. Visibility affected.	11·30	16·0
12	64+	Hurricane	The air is filled with foam and spray. Sea completely white with driving spray; visibility very seriously affected.	13·70	—

Even on the calmest days there will be little waves lapping the shore, and movement on the sea's surface. Somewhere in the world the wind is blowing, and that wind encourages ocean currents which heap the surface water into waves, carrying their ripple effect for thousands of miles from sea to sea. Wind force is precisely measured by an anemometer, but everyone with an interest in sea conditions can make a rough estimate. The scale is quite easy to learn and very useful.

A different kind of movement in the sea is caused by the tides. Tides are brought about by the gravitational pull of the Sun and Moon on the Earth. Sometimes they work together; sometimes against each other. In response to these changing forces, the level of the sea rises and falls in tides which vary greatly from the time of new or full moon, to the quarters. The greatest effect of all is at the time of the spring and autumn *equinoxes*. At new and full moons the extra-high tides are called *spring tides*. At quarters, the smaller variations are known as *neap tides*.

Just under the surface, the sea is teeming with life. Millions of tiny plants and animals – *plankton* – float and drift, providing food for larger creatures. Young fish of all sorts, like herrings and pilchards and mackerel, hunt the plankton pastures and are in turn hunted by sharks and whales.

There is endless battle and carnage near the surface, and a rain of debris falls onto the sea bed where bottom-dwellers like crabs, lobsters and flatfish live on this food and on one another. Clouds of spores or eggs rise to enrich the plankton and maintain the cycle. Birds, paddling on the surface or diving out of the sky, scoop or stab the fish. Man trawls, nets and hooks. Large creatures feed on smaller ones, but all die eventually, their bodies providing food for others. Nothing is wasted.

N.W.C.

8

Violet Sea Snail
Janthina janthina

By-the-wind-Sailor
Velella velella

Some animals spend their whole lives drifting, though they may be cast ashore to die on the tide-line. Many start in warmer latitudes and reach the coast of Britain as strays carried by the North Atlantic Current. The *Portugese Man-O-War* is an example, sometimes reaching south-western waters in large numbers. An air-filled bladder acts as a sail so that the jellyfish is driven by winds as well as currents. Its tentacles sting and paralyse fish to provide food.

Velella, or *Jack-by-the-Wind*, has a thin half-disc sail, which drives the jellyfish along, tentacles trailing. The sail is set at an angle to the 'hull', and the young jellyfish are born to sail either on the port or the starboard tack, so that at least half of them won't end up on the nearest beach! The violet sea snail, *Janthina*, is a sea-going mollusc which floats on a raft of foamy bubbles, living in the open ocean but sometimes carried to our waters by currents.

Jellyfish
Chrysaora hysoscella

Portugese man-o'-war
Physalia physalis

Shipworm
Teredo navalis

Goose Barnacle
Lepas antifera

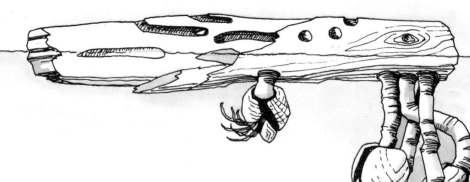

Another snail, the shipworm, burrows into floating timber while still a larva. As it grows, it tunnels deeper, feeding both on the sea and the cellulose of the wood it lives in. This tunnelling caused many wooden ships to sink before anti-fouling paint and copper-plating were devised. Goose-barnacles, *Lepas*, were almost as unwelcome in sailing-ship days. They don't damage planking, but slow the vessel by breaking the smooth lines of the hull below water.

Some jellyfish are able to move along by jet-propulsion and so maintain their position in the surface feeding grounds. *Aurelia* is the most common jellyfish, with violet oval marks on the upper side of the bell. *Chrysaora* is orange-brown, while *Rhizostoma* is football-sized and mushroom-shaped. All these feed on plankton and small fish and are apt to sting you if you swim too close!

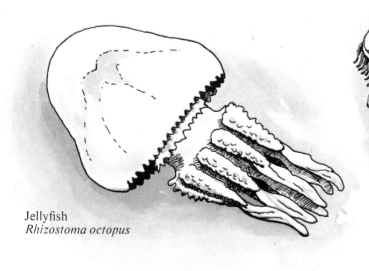

Jellyfish
Rhizostoma octopus

Jellyfish
Aurelia aurita
N.W.C.

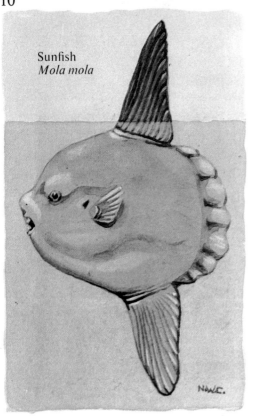

Sunfish
Mola mola

NoWC.

Fish are unable to breathe air, but extract oxygen from the water by using their gills. They are superbly designed for an underwater life, but they can often be detected on the surface when they rise to feed.

The herring, once caught in great numbers in the North Sea by drifters from Yarmouth and Lowestoft, has been overfished there and become scarce. Mackerel in shoals, chasing fry near the coast in summer, sometimes make the sea seem almost to boil by their activity. These commotions attract gannets, terns and sometimes porpoises. There are shoals of grey mullet off our coasts in summer too and these move up river estuaries with the tide. They may be found grazing on algae from a boat's bottom as she rides at anchor. Bass are fish much sought by sea-anglers, and they, too, come to our shores only in summer. Dogfish are small sharks. They live on the sea bottom and are sometimes found in crab pots. When caught by trawlers, the lesser spotted dogfish appears in the fish-monger's as 'rock salmon'. Plaice are also bottom dwellers, well camouflaged as they lie among the stones and gravel. They are one of those curious fish which, as they grow, become one-sided – flattened so that they lie on the sea bottom on their left side, the eye from that side moves to the upper-most right side, giving an odd, twisted look to the head.

The sunfish is a large fish from tropical waters which drifts with ocean currents, like jellyfish and plankton, and sometimes appears off the south-western shores of Britain. The tip of its dorsal fin shows above water as it earns its name, seeming to bask in the sun. The fin may be mistaken for a shark's but is quite a different shape.

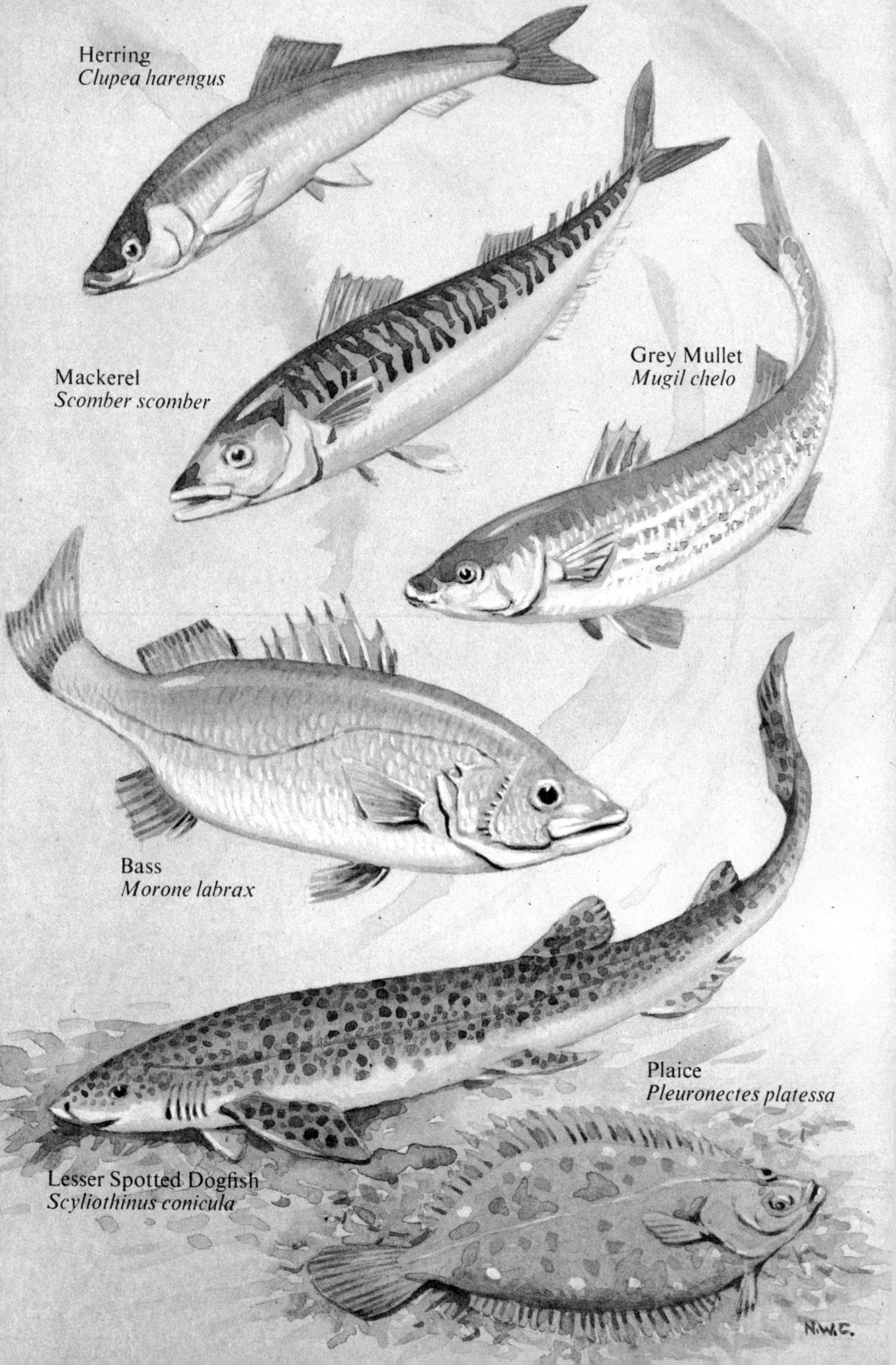

Herring
Clupea harengus

Mackerel
Scomber scomber

Grey Mullet
Mugil chelo

Bass
Morone labrax

Plaice
Pleuronectes platessa

Lesser Spotted Dogfish
Scyliothinus conicula

N.W.E.

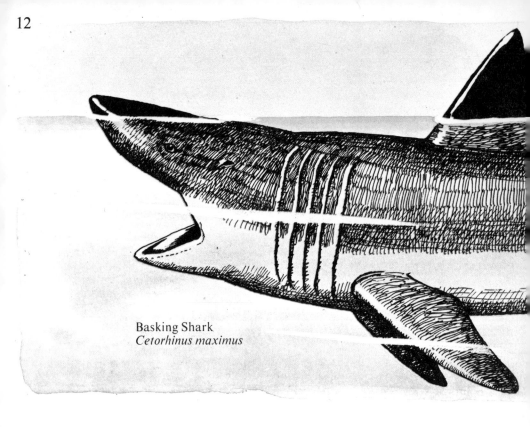

Basking Shark
Cetorhinus maximus

The harmless and magnificent basking shark is almost the largest
fish in the world, second only to the tropical white shark. Measuring
up to twelve metres in length, its gets its name from its habit of
lying motionless at the surface, enjoying the sun. Nobody knows
where they spend the winter but they appear off our south-western
coasts in May or June and move slowly north, until they may be
seen off Norway in August. Then they disappear, possibly to
hibernate.

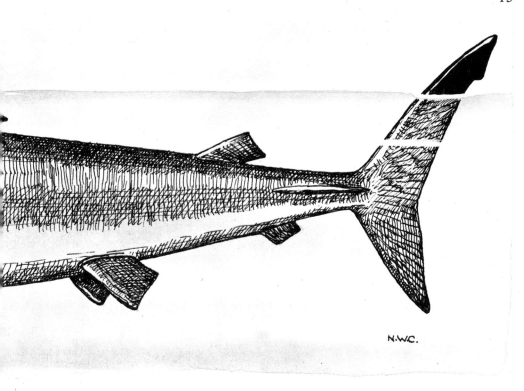

N.W.C.

Sometimes alone, sometimes with one or two others, sometimes in parties of anything up to a hundred, the basking shark cruises inshore, swimming sluggishly along and with its blunt snout, dorsal fin and the upper part of the tail fin breaking the surface. Huge though it is, it feeds entirely on plankton. It swims with open mouth, drawing in vast quantities of sea which pass out through its gills. The plankton is filtered by a sieve-like structure formed by inter-locking gill-rakes, like the teeth of a comb. At the speed of two knots it is said to sieve the seafood from fifteen hundred tons of water in one hour! It has no swim-bladder and gains buoyancy from its massive oily liver, which weighs a quarter as much as the whole fish. This liver was formerly in demand for its oil, and shark fisheries operated on the coasts of Scotland and Ireland. One liver yielded about 125 gallons. The basking shark's indifference to people is remarkable, so it can easily be harpooned. Divers can swim close to a cruising shark and the only real danger is that a startled or injured fish may damage man or boat by a lash of its powerful tail

Arctic Skua
dark form

Sandwich Tern

Arctic Skua
light form

Many kinds of birds make a living as fishermen. None is adapted to a totally marine life, as they have no way of nesting and incubating eggs at sea.

The most obvious sea birds are the gulls. Except for the kittiwake, which outside the breeding season is truly oceanic, gulls are coastal creatures. They are scavengers. They have flourished with the spread of man and his activities, following him inland to sewage farms and rubbish tips, as well as frequenting fishing harbours. The black-headed gull, which is black-headed only in summer, is just as likely to be seen inland as by the shore or at sea. This is the gull that follows the plough for worms.

Young gulls are more or less brown and may not achieve the adult grey and white plumage until they are three or four years old. In adults, bill and leg colours are helpful identification marks.

Skuas look rather hawkish. They are more or less brown, and can be confused with immature gulls. They are pirates among sea birds and, like gulls, they are scavengers, but they are also agile and aggressive thieves. They get much of their food by chasing other birds, particularly terns, forcing them to drop their catch and then grabbing it.

Great Black-backed Gull
Adult

Kittiwake
Adult

Great Black-backed Gull
Juvenile

Lesser Black-backed Gull
Adult

Kittiwake
Juvenile

Lesser Black-backed Gull
Juvenile

Herring Gull
Adult

Herring Gull
Juvenile

Common Gull
Adult

Common Gull
Juvenile

Black-headed Gull
Summer Adult

Black-headed Gull
Winter Adult

Black-headed Gull
Juvenile

Gannet

Gannet

Gannets and terns are plunge divers. They first spot their fish from the air, then close their wings to accelerate in a headlong splash and chase. Specially adapted for plunge diving, with slit nostrils and protective air-sacs forming a double breast, gannets strike the surface with great force, sending up a tremendous splash and continuing the dive in an underwater chase using feet and wings. The catch may be swallowed underwater or it may be brought to the surface. Usually the dive is brief and the bird rises, takes off, circles and dives again. Though you may see them close inshore, especially in stormy weather, they are usually far out to sea. Whiter-than-white, long wings tipped with black, they are as big as a turkey, and easily recognised.

Terns, or sea swallows, are small and graceful; they hover, with head pointing down, using their forked tails for balance, choosing from the fish fry before they plunge. They are quite likely to be found close inshore, often feeding in very shallow water. They do not dive deep, and often pick their prey from the surface without getting their feet wet. The best way to identify terns is by their bill colour, though it is difficult to tell the difference between common and arctic terns. Gannets are silent fishermen, while terns chatter with shrill calls.

Little Tern

Sandwich Tern

Gannet

Arctic Tern

Common Tern

Gannet

N.W.C.

Shag

Razorbill

Pictured opposite are birds which swim a lot and dive in pursuit of fish. Cormorants and shags are common around the coast of Britain and are seldom seen out of sight of land. The shag frequents rocky shores, whereas the cormorant is also found in estuaries and even on inland lakes. The cormorant's white throat and thigh patch, like the shag's crest, are brief adornments of the courtship period. Both swim low in the water and dive from the surface, often with a jack-knife leap. They then pursue their prey underwater propelled by their broad webbed feet and with the help of half-open wings. Both have a habit of standing on rocks or posts with wings spread, apparently to dry, after diving.

On the cliffs, auks seem clumsy and ill at ease, but in the sea they are fine divers. They catch their fish, mostly small fry, by 'flying' underwater. They spend a great deal of time on the surface paddling about, dipping their heads in the sea and sometimes 'standing up' and shaking their wings. They can fly well when they want to, their long narrow wings flapping quickly, whirring their short stout bodies through the air.

Cormorant

Shag

Shag

Puffin
Winter

Puffins
Summer

Guillemot
Winter

Guillemot
Summer

Tystie
Winter

Tystie
Summer

Razorbill
Winter

Razorbill
Summer

N.W.CUSA.

The birds most adapted to a marine existence are the 'tube-noses'. The largest of these are the Albatrosses, birds of southern seas that are seen in British waters only as rare vagrants. One British tube-nose is the fulmar, which has become very common in the last 30 years, having spread from a few colonies on islands north of Scotland to almost every suitable cliff in Britain. This is believed to be due to increased fishing by man providing more offal cast overboard from boats. The fulmar is a truly marine bird, visiting land only to breed. At first sight it can easily be taken for a gull but it is really quite different, with no black in the wing tips; thick-set and bull-necked, it has the characteristic rigid-winged gliding albatross flight. The most common shearwater in British waters, and the only one to breed in Britain, is the Manx shearwater. It is a more slender bird than the fulmar, black above and white below, but with the same stiff-winged, banking flight.

The storm-petrel flutters over the waves, butterfly fashion. It often follows boats, which the manx shearwater does not, but they both nest in old burrows and crannies, often on the same islands.

Eiders, scoters and mergansers are sea ducks, which breed in Scotland, but may be found around English shores, especially in sheltered waters in winter-time. Mergansers, and particular divers, are solitary birds.

Eider
Male

Eider
Female

Common Scoter
Male

Red-throated
Diver
Winter

Great Northern Diver
Winter

Fulmar

Manx
Shearwater

Wandering Albatross

Storm Petrel

Red-breasted
Merganser
Female

Common Scoter
Female

Red-breasted Merganser
Male

N.W.C.

Atlantic Grey Seal

Besides birds there are other warm-blooded animals living in the sea, but these are mammals, creatures which suckle their young. Seals, which come ashore to rest and to bear their young are mammals. There are two categories, true seals and sea-lions, but there are no sea-lions in British waters. In true seals the hind limbs have become flippers extending backwards from the rear of the body, whereas in sea-lions they can be swung forward like legs. So sea-lions are quite nimble on land while the true seal is a sausage of blubber that can move only in an ungainly fashion by a caterpillar-like undulation of its body, aided by the fore-flippers. It may be clumsy on land but when it takes to the water its stream-lined, insulated body is driven rapidly by sweeps of the hind flippers; no longer the useless paws of the land, but powerful propellers. Seals eat fish and spend much of their time under the surface for, although they breathe air, they are adapted so that they can stay below as much as an hour. Their nostrils and ears close as soon as they submerge. At times they sleep underwater, rising to the surface occasionally to breathe and then sinking again.

At sea, seals feel secure in their ability to dive in a flash with a slap of their hind-flippers, becoming ghostly dark streaks in the depths. Besides the occasional wanderers of exotic species, two seals are common in British waters. These are the grey or Atlantic seal and the common or harbour seal. The common seal is found on the east coast of England and in Scotland. Generally it prefers estuaries with sand banks, whereas the grey seal, which is the more common seal in the west, prefers rocky shores. The young of the common seal are born on sand banks and can swim away on the tide in a matter of hours. The white new-born pups of the grey seal almost always remain on the beach or near it for about a month. They are are usually born on inaccessible beaches at the foot of steep cliffs, or in remote sea-caves. Grey seals are the larger and have Roman noses (especially the bulls), while common seals have dished, dog-like faces. Both are more or less spotted.

Common Seal

N.W.C.

Killer Whale

Pilot Whale

Killer Whale   N.W.C.

Like seals, whales are mammals, but they are more completely adapted to sea life, suckling their young underwater and never venturing ashore. If they go too near to the shore, and get stranded, they die. There are two broad categories, whale-bone whales and toothed whales.

Whale-bone whales are immense but harmless creatures. Like the basking shark they live on plankton. The whale bone or *baleen* consists of a row of fringed plates in the mouth which act as sieves collecting minute life from the sea water. The lesser rorqual is probably the most common of the whale-bone whales in British waters, and can be as much as 10 metres long. Toothed whales, as their name suggests, live on larger prey, such as fish, and one of them, the killer whale or grampus, which is not uncommon around these islands, also devours seals, birds, and smaller whales. They hunt in packs as a rule but are probably harmless to man, although to be in a small boat and eyed by one or two of these monsters must be disconcerting to say the least. The grampus has a bold black and white pattern and a dorsal fin as much as two metres tall in an old male. The pilot whale, caa'ing whale or blackfish, is also a toothed whale. In the Faeroe Islands a watch is kept for the large 'schools' of these animals, and they are rounded up by men in small boats armed with spears, and driven ashore to provide meat.

Bottle-nosed Dolphin

Common Dolphin

White-sided Dolphin

White-beaked Dolphin

H.W.C.

Dolphins are small whales – warm-blooded creatures more closely related to you and me than to the fish they look so much like. Fish shape is the best shape for travelling through water. The dolphin's streamlined body hardly disturbs the water, and its skin has a thick layer of blubber which keeps it warm. Dolphins are about $2\frac{1}{2}$ to $3\frac{1}{2}$ metres long. They have beaks which, while they are easy enough to see in drawings and marine zoos, are rarely seen above water at sea. They are fish-eaters, with powerful jaws and sharp teeth. Their nostrils are on top of their heads, so that they can breathe as soon as they break the surface.

Dolphins are sociable animals, travelling in 'schools'. A rough way of guessing the number in a school is to count the dorsal fins showing above water at any one time and then to multiply by five. They are inquisitive, and are much attracted to boats and even to bathers in shallow water, though when this happens it is usually a single animal which for some reason has become separated from its fellows. Following power boats, dolphins jostle for a place on the bow wave, using its lift for a free ride. They will also investigate yachts, often staying for a while to fascinate the watching sailors.

Dolphins have beaks, porpoises do not. In our waters, we are only likely to see the common porpoise. It is less than two metres long – stout and robust, black on the back and white underneath. A coastal species, it can travel up estuaries, chasing mackerel and mullet, and has often been caught in salmon nets.

Porpoises

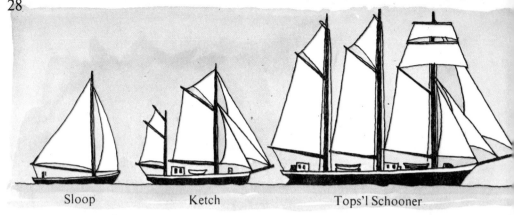

Sloop Ketch Tops'l Schooner

Ships come in all shapes and sizes, to do a variety of different jobs, but their underwater shapes are remarkably similar, being more or less fish-like, however different they may be above the waterline. In order to travel, and not merely to float, they need power. In the past this was provided by the wind blowing on a foil-shaped sail similar in design to a bird's wing. Nowadays, ships are driven by the rotating blades of a propeller, or *screw*, which is a development of the sweeping motion of a fish fin. Most small sailing boats are fore-and-aft rigged, sloops with a single mast and ketches with two masts, though there are still many gaff-rigged boats about to please the eye, and the occasional sail-training topsail schooner.

Commercial ships are designed to carry cargo or passengers, or sometimes both. Cargo ships differ in shape according to the nature of the load. An oil tanker has a cat-walk above the tanks and the funnel and crew-housing are usually at the rear. Much modern freight is moved in containers and ships have been specially designed to carry these huge standard-sized crates. Cargo vessels are usually fitted with derricks for loading and unloading. The lights of large, handsome passenger ships, arrayed with portholes, glitter across the sea at night.

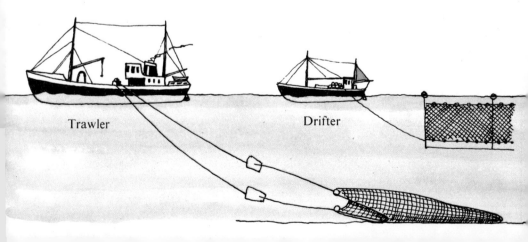

Trawler Drifter

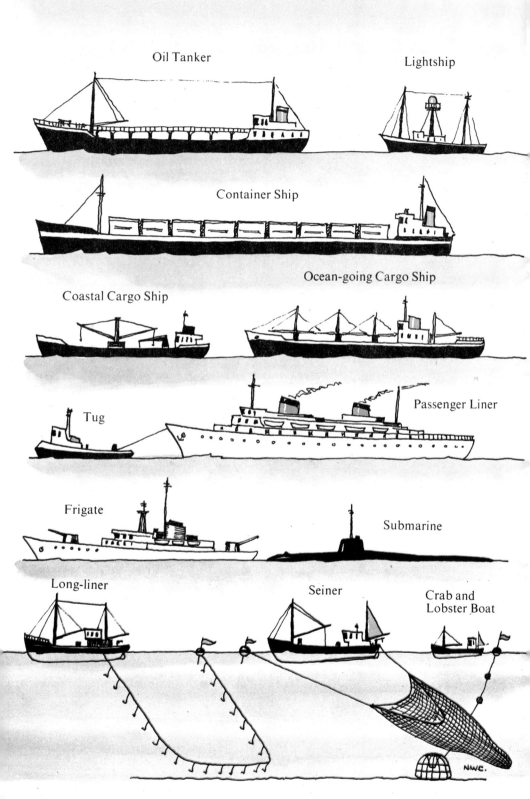

Oil Tanker

Lightship

Container Ship

Ocean-going Cargo Ship

Coastal Cargo Ship

Tug

Passenger Liner

Frigate

Submarine

Long-liner

Seiner

Crab and
Lobster Boat

Tugs are small, powerful vessels busy in harbours and inshore waters, guiding larger vessels through the safe channels, with the crew-quarters well to the fore and towing gear amidships. Warships are grey, and bristle with a complexity of electronic gear in solid upperworks. Submarines are usually black and, when seen low on the surface, cormorant-like, inconspicous and sinister.

Fishing vessels are among the most attractive ships, their design perfected by thousands of years of severe testing in every weather. Every fitting and every inch of space has its function, and the ship is supremely adapted to its job. She is always in direct competition with animal fishermen, so it is only just that fish and birds gain from the fisherman's activities. If you see a fishing boat surrounded by birds, she is either hauling her nets or the catch is being gutted. Either way, there is bound to be a lot of food around for birds, and for fish as well, as the offal sinks. On the surface you are likely to see great black-backed and herring gulls, if the land is not far away. Further out to sea, there's a chance of anything from a gannet to a fulmar, storm petrel or kittiwake, all jostling for a meal.

Lighthouses are good places for seawatching. They are often built on headlands or points of land reaching into the sea — spots were both boats and birds tend to pass close inshore on their journeys.

Herring Gull

Fulmar

Returning Trawler

Kittiwakes
Winter Adults

Kittiwake
Juvenile

On a calm night in late summer you may sometimes see one of the magical performances of nature. As the wavelets lap along the shore their line is marked by a splash of pale greenish light. Or, in a boat, the bow wave and the wash may sparkle with curious flashes and the water drips from paddle blades as if afire. Tiny animals, called flagellates, are present in the sea in enormous numbers. When they are agitated or disturbed, they glow with phosphorescent and produce a firework display that will never be forgotten.